An internal – combustion engine is a heat e[ngine]... converted from the heat of burning gasoline into mechanical work, or torque.

That torque is applied to the wheels so as to make the car move.

Unless you are driving an ancient two – stroke Saab (which sounds like an old chain saw and belches oily smoke out of its exhaust), your engine works on the same basic principles whether you're wheeling a Ford or a Ferrari.

Engines have pistons that move up and down inside metal tubes called cylinders.

Imagine riding a bicycle: Your legs move up and down to turn the pedals.

Pistons are connected via rods (they're like your shins) to a crankshaft, they move up and down to spin the engine's crankshaft, the same way your legs spin the bike's – which in turn powers the bike's drive wheel or car's drive wheels.

Depending on the vehicle, there are typically between 2 and 12 cylinders in the engine, with a piston moving up and down in each Cylinder.

Engine Parts

Engine Block

Or Cylinder block is a metal casting that contains the piston cylinders and cooling ducts of an engine.

Each car has one engine block.

There are many types of engine block, inline and V types are the most common thanks to their efficiency.

Inline engines have their cylinders arranged in a single row, for up to six cylinders.

V engines have their cylinders arranged in two banks, forming an angle, their overwhelming use today is for six or eight cylinders.

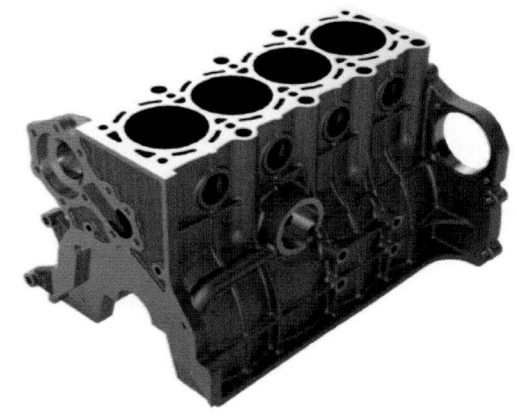

inline 4 cylinder block

v8 cylinder block

Engine Head

Or the cylinder head (often informally abbreviated to just head), sits above the cylinders on top of the cylinder block.

It closes at the top of the cylinder, forming the combustion chamber.

In most engines, the head also provides space for the passages that convey air and fuel to the cylinder. They also allow the escaping of the exhaust. Moreover, the valves, spark plugs, and fuel injectors can be mounted on the engine head.

Note: A " V " engine has two-cylinder heads.

**3 cylinder Head
(below view)**

**4 cylinder head
(below and above views)**

Head gasket

There are three fluids, which travel between the engine block and the cylinder head:

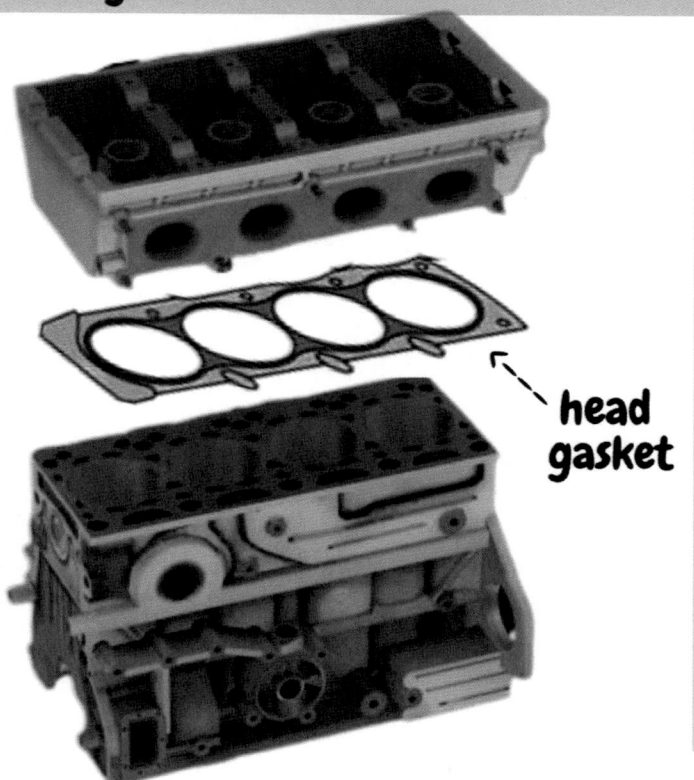

head gasket

1- Combustion gases (unburned air / fuel mixture and exhaust gases) in each cylinder.

2- Water - based coolant in the coolant passages.

3- Lubricating oil in the oil galleries.

Correct operation of the engine requires that each of these circuits do not leak or lose pressure at the junction of the engine block and the cylinder head.

The head gasket is the seal that prevents these leaks and pressure losses.

Valve cover and crankcase

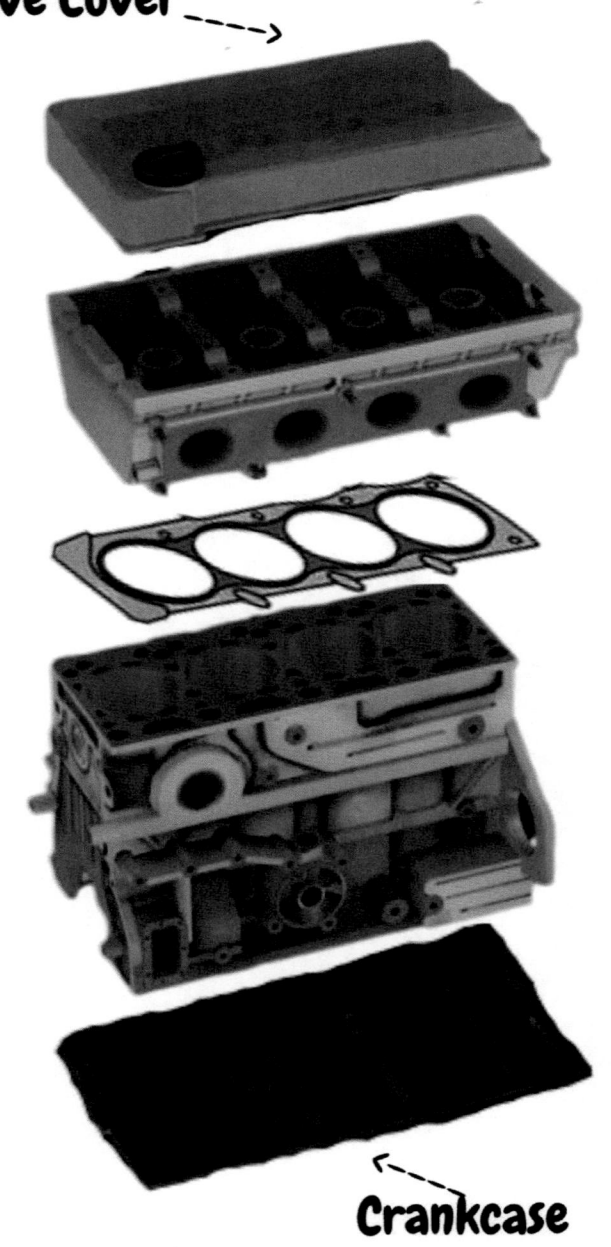

Valve Cover ---->

Crankcase

Valve Cover

Valve cover (or cylinder head cover) is particularly used for covering a cylinder head of an internal combustion engine has a plurality of functional elements such as an oil filling connection and at least one oil separation device mounted thereon.

Crankcase

A crankcase is the housing for the crankshaft in a reciprocating internal combustion engine.
In most modern engines, the crankcase is integrated into the engine block.

Crankshaft

A crankshaft is a shaft driven by a crank mechanism. It consists of a series of cranks and crankpins to which the connecting rods of an engine are attached.

The crankshaft is driven by a piston group. It transfers torque to the flywheel, which in turn rotates the gears of the transmission. Further, the rotation is transmitted on the drive axles.

All cars equipped with an internal combustion engine contains such a mechanism.

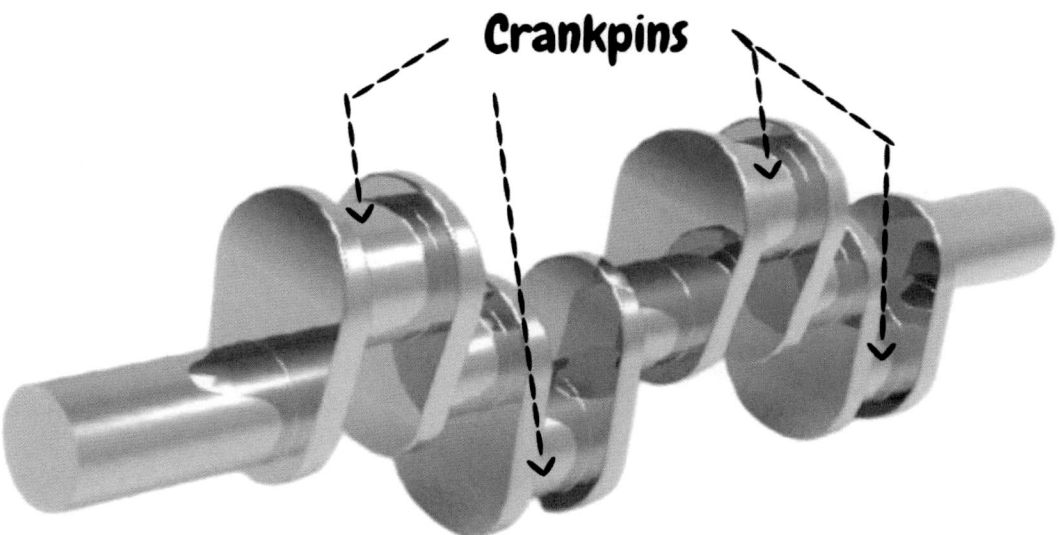

Crankpins

Inline four cylinder crankshaft

Connecting rod

A connecting rod, also called a con rod, is a part of the piston engine that connects the piston to the crankshaft. Simultaneously with the crank.

The connecting rod converts, the reciprocating motion of the piston into the rotation of the crankshaft.

Piston

The internal combustion engine uses one or more pistons to convert pressure into a rotational motion.

It is the moving component contained in a cylinder and is made gas-tight by piston rings.

The same principles are found in most automobiles.

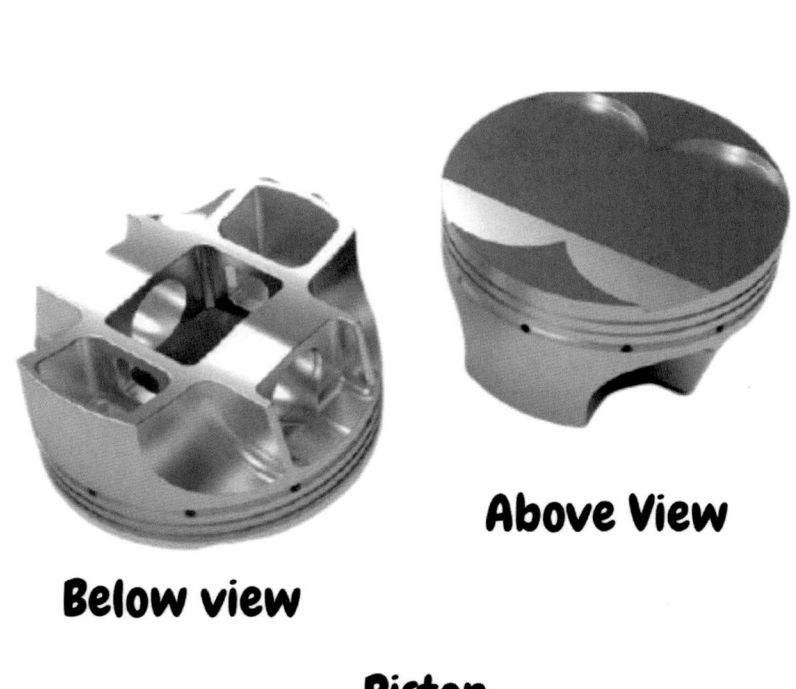

Below view

Above View

Piston

Pistonn + connecting rod

Inline four cylinder piston + connecting rod + crankshaft.

V8 cylinder piston + connecting rod + crankshaft.

Valve

valves are mechanical components used to control the timing and quantity of gas or vapor flow into an engine.

The valve is usually a metallic flat disk with a long rod known as the "valve stem".

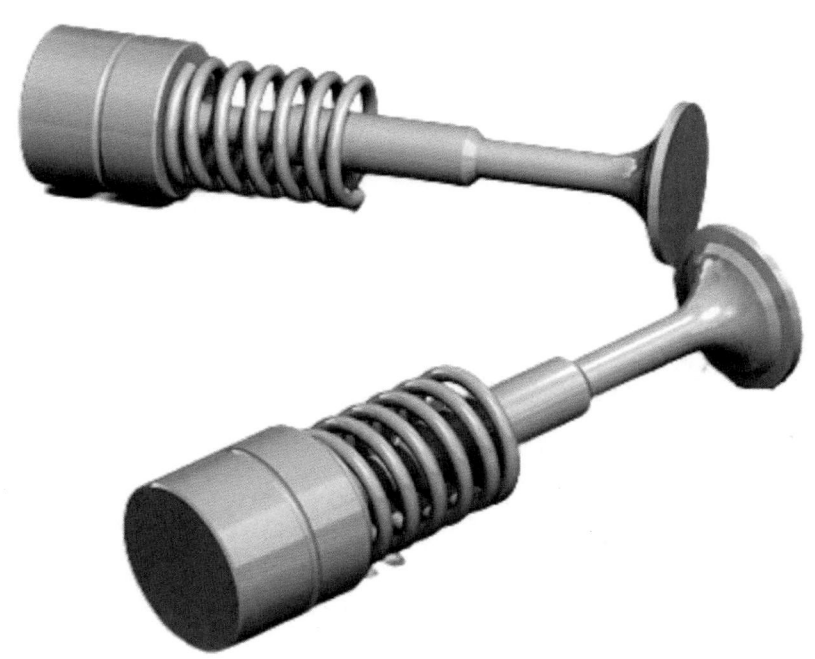

The valve is used to open and close the intake and exhaust ports in the cylinder head.

valves from below.

valves from above.

inline 4 cylinder head + valves

This engine has two valves per cylinder, there is also, multivalve engine where each cylinder has more than two valves. It may have three, four, or five valves per cylinder.

Some engines have one intake and one exhaust valve, some engines have two intakes and one exhaust valve.
Usually, high performance engines use two intakes and exhaust valves.

Camshaft

A camshaft is a rotating object usually made of metal. It consists of several radial cams.

Camshafts are used in internal combustion engines (to operate the intake and exhaust valves).

They are a key factor in determining the RPM range of an engine's power band.

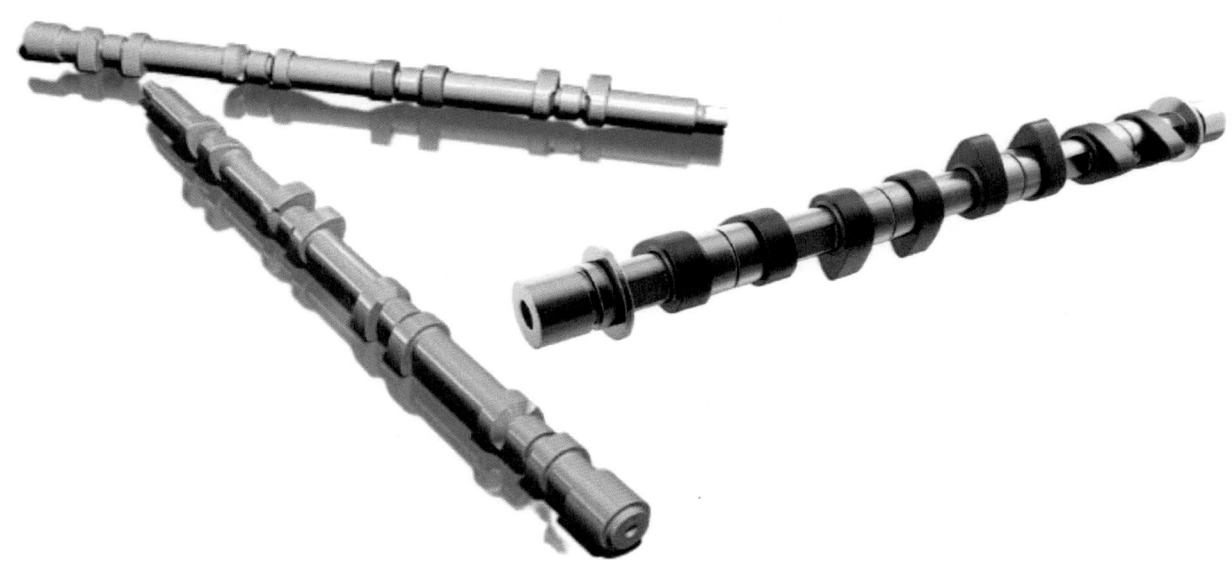

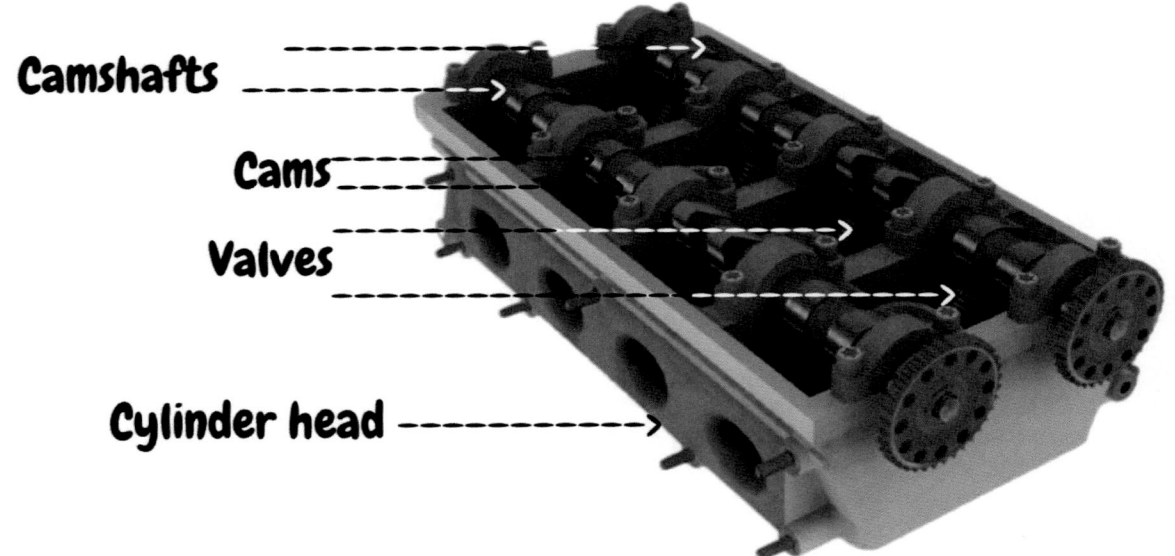

Camshafts

Cams

Valves

Cylinder head

Double overhead camshafts, 4 cylinder inline engine

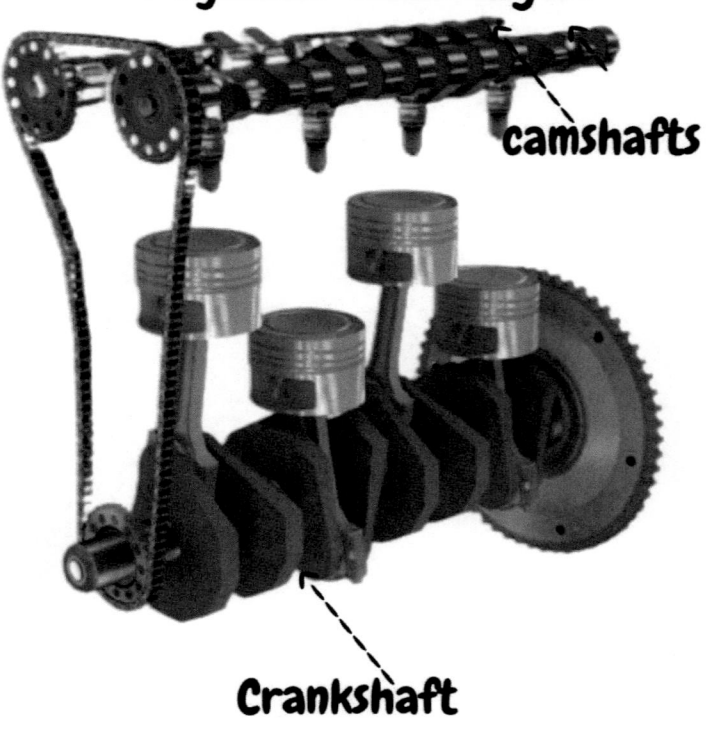

camshafts

The camshaft is connected to the crankshaft via a belt, a chain or gears.

This ensures the consistent timing of the valves in relation to the motion of the pistons.

Crankshaft

Single overhead camshaft

The oldest configuration of overhead camshaft engine is the single overhead camshaft (SOHC) design.

A SOHC engine has one camshaft per bank of cylinders, therefore a straight engine has no more than one camshaft.

A V or flat engine with a total of two camshafts (one per bank of cylinders) is a single overhead camshaft engine.

Double overhead camshaft

A double overhead camshaft or dual overhead camshaft (DOHC or "twin-cam") engine has two camshafts per bank of cylinder head, one for the intake valves and the other for the exhaust valves.

Therefore there are two camshafts for a straight engine and a total of four camshafts for a V engine or a flat engine.

Injector & Spark plug

Fuel injectors are parts of modern car engines that deliver fuel to the engine's combustion chamber, directly or indirectly.

These small electro-mechanical devices are typically positioned at a certain angle to make sure that the fuel is sprayed towards the engine's inlet valve or directly into the cylinder.

Injector

A spark plug is a device for delivering electric current from an ignition system to the combustion chamber, to ignite the compressed fuel/air mixture by an electric spark. While containing combustion pressure within the engine.

Spark plugs are used in the petrol engines to ignite the air fuel mixture whereas in diesel engines the presence of spark plugs is not necessary.

Spark plug

Overview

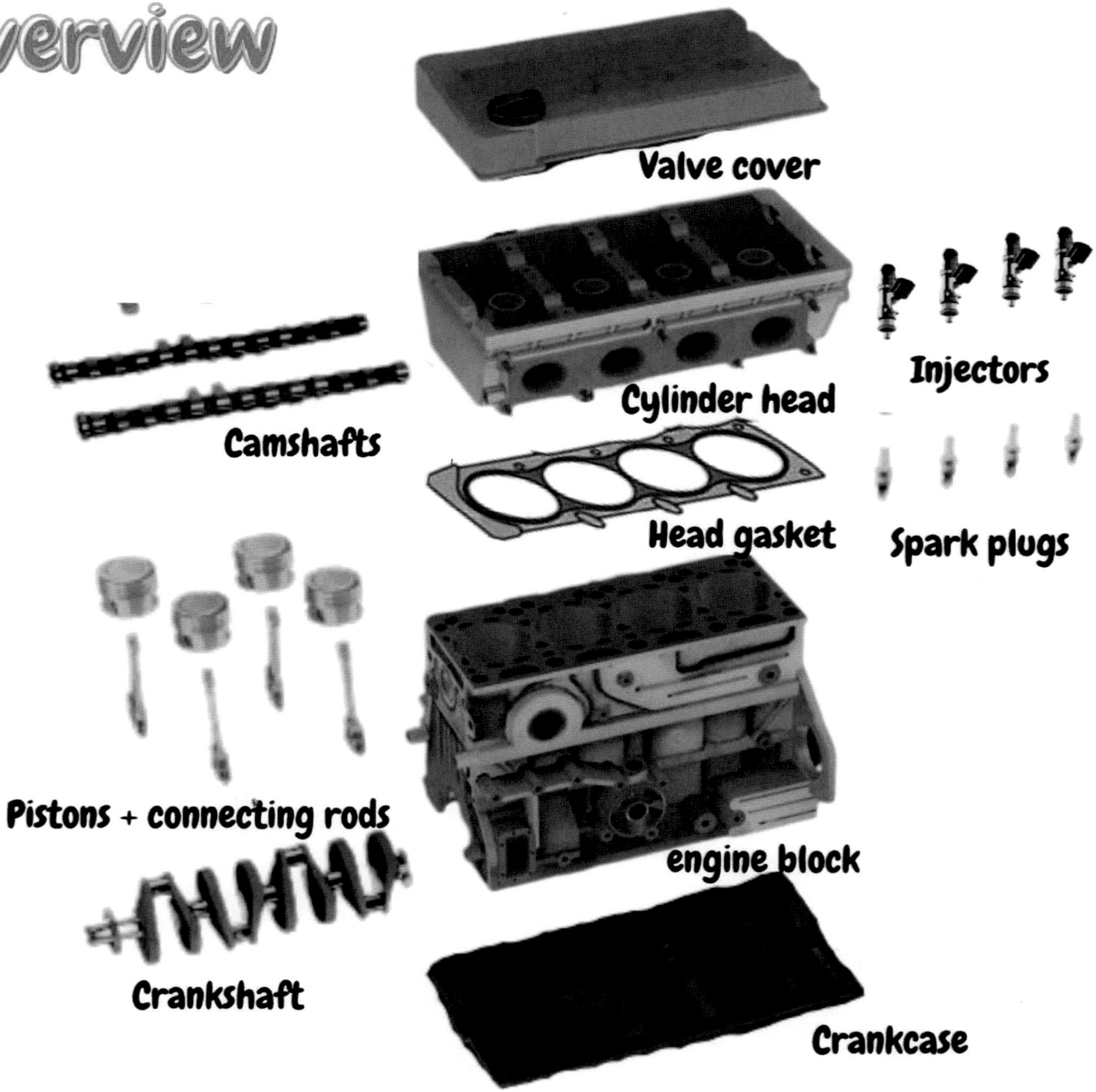

Valve cover

Cylinder head

Injectors

Camshafts

Head gasket

Spark plugs

Pistons + connecting rods

engine block

Crankshaft

Crankcase

The moving parts

The moving parts of an engine serve an important function in turning heat energy into mechanical energy.

Moreover, they convert reciprocal motion into rotary motion.

The principal moving parts are:

The piston.

Connecting rods.

Crankshaft.

Camshaft.

Valves.

and Gear train.

Valve cover, Cylinder head, Head gasket, Engine block, Crankcase and spark plugs are non-moving parts.

Assembly

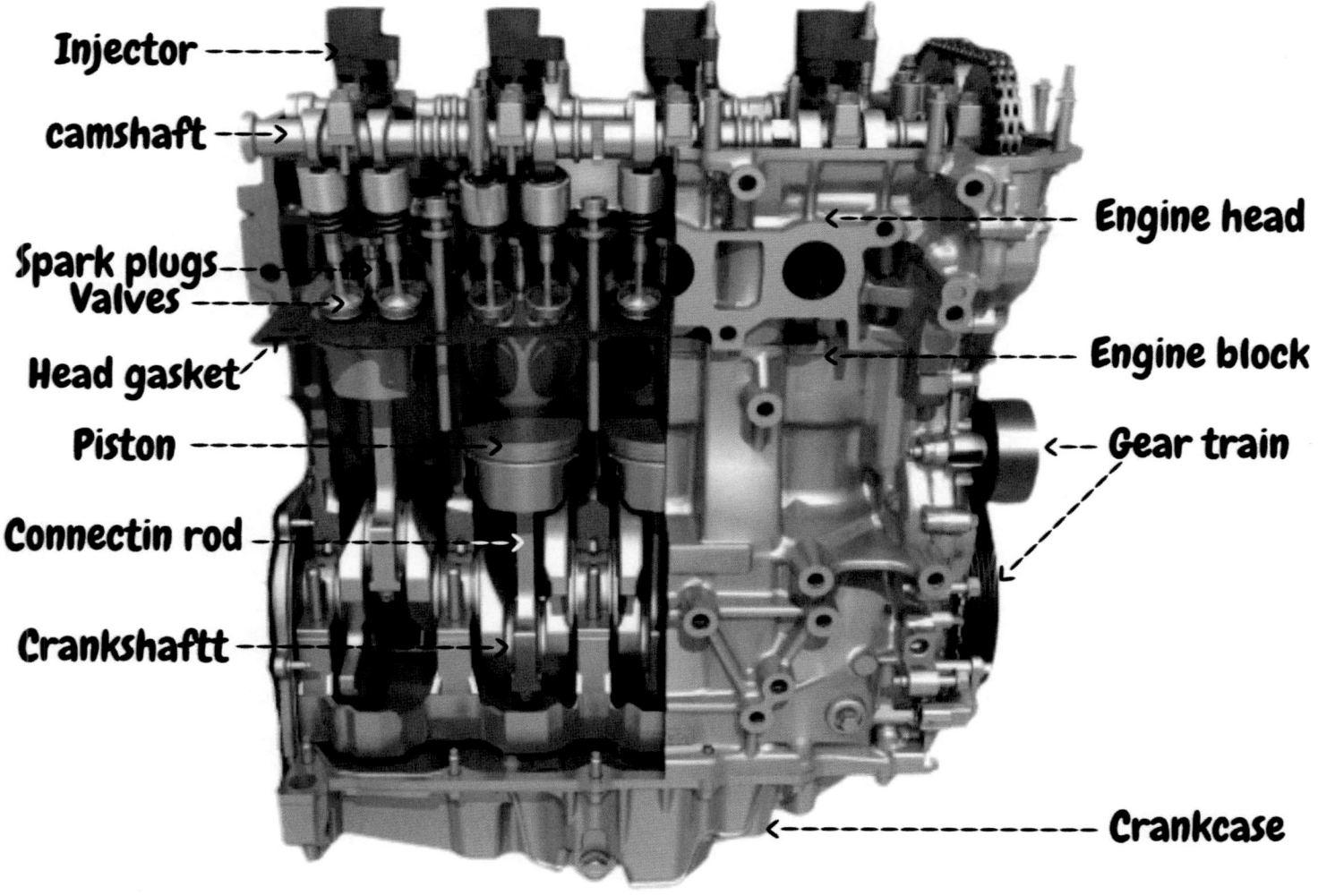

Injector
camshaft
Spark plugs
Valves
Head gasket
Piston
Connectin rod
Crankshaftt

Engine head
Engine block
Gear train
Crankcase

Inline 4 cylinder engine, Double overhead camshaft..

V8 cylinder engine,

Dual-overhead, two camshafts per bank of cylinder.

First engine view, for crankshaft, pistons, engine head, valves and spark plugs.

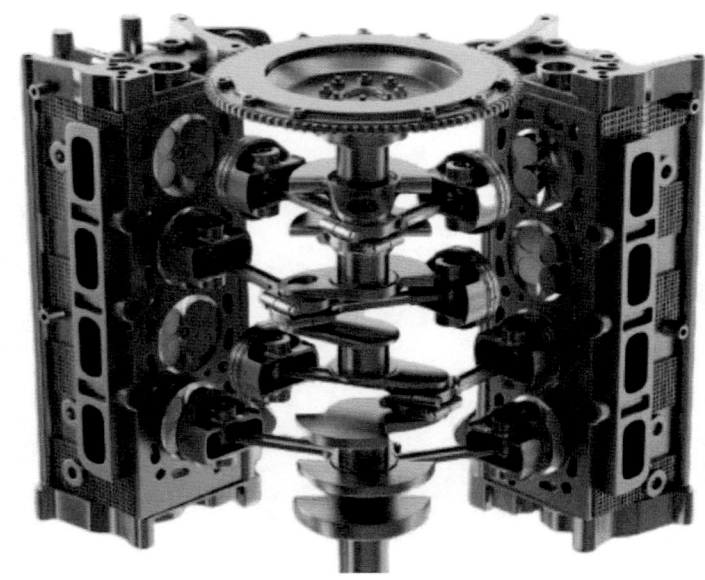

And this is a second view of the same engine with a crankcase and without engine heads.

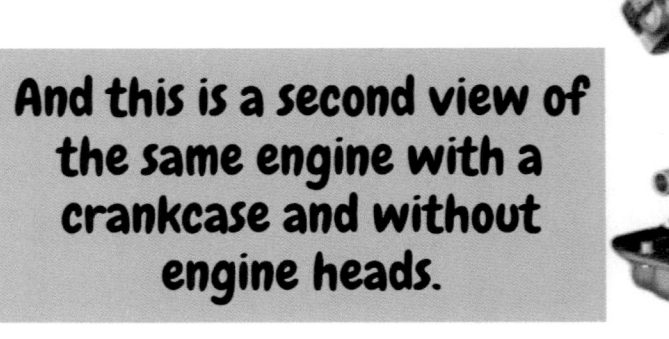

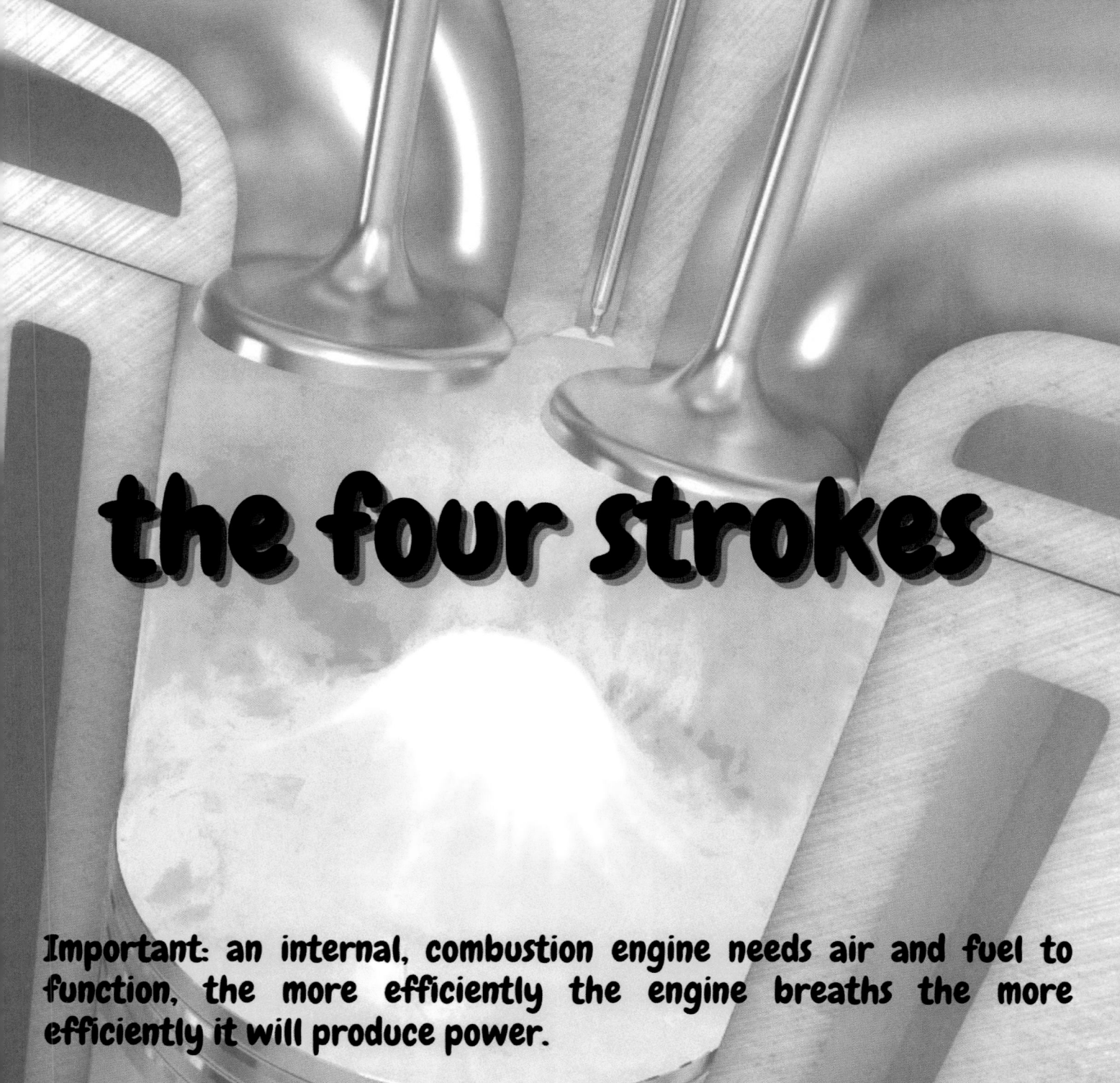

the four strokes

Important: an internal, combustion engine needs air and fuel to function, the more efficiently the engine breaths the more efficiently it will produce power.

Bore and Stroke

An engine's stroke is the distance the piston travels inside the cylinder (from BDC to TDC).

TDC: top dead center.   **BDC: bottom dead center.**

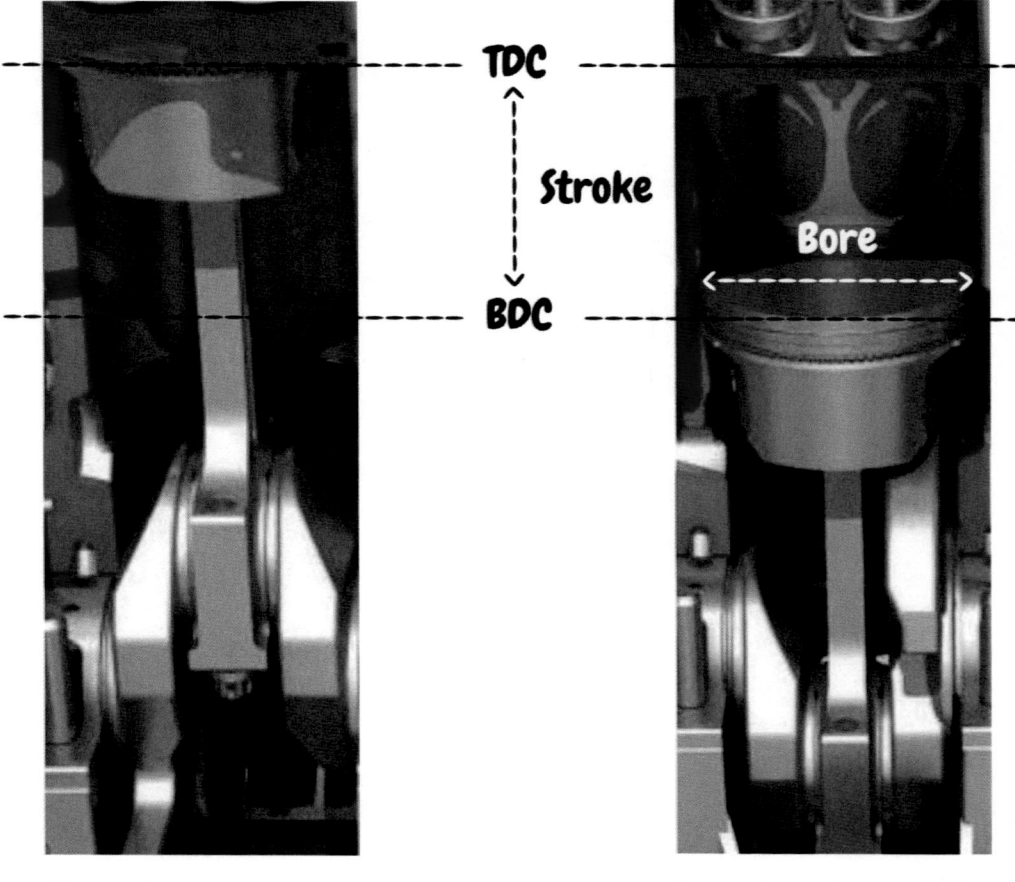

Crank angel 0°   Crank angel 180°

The crankshaft makes one revolution while the piston moves from the top of the cylinder to the bottom and back to the top.

Since the piston is connected to the crankshaft, we can note the movement of the piston by the rotation angle of the crankshaft.

Zero degrees occurs when the piston is at the top of the cylinder. Since there are 360 degrees in one revolution, the piston is at the bottom when the crank angle is 180 degrees.

The distance traveled by the piston from zero degrees to 180 degrees is called the stroke – S of the piston.

This explains why modern automobile engines are called four-stroke engines. The piston makes four strokes and the crankshaft makes two revolutions.

(This means that the crankshaft must go around twice, and each piston moves up and down two times).

The diameter of the piston, and the inside diameter of the cylinder, is called the bore – B.

So the area A of the head of the piston is pi (3.14159) times the diameter squared divided by four.

$$A = (pi * B\text{\textasciicircum}2) / 4$$

The volume swept out during any complete stroke is the piston area times the stroke – S:

$$V = (pi * S * B\text{\textasciicircum}2)/ 4 = A * S$$

This volume is called the working fluid volume because the work performed by a moving gas under pressure is equal to the pressure of the gas times the volume of the moved gas.

Total displacement (D) :

$$D= V * N$$

    V = working volume.
    N = number of cylinders

for example : 2.4 Liter 4 cylinder engine, has V=0.6 Liter .

$$D = V * 4 = 2.4 \text{ Liter}$$

A four stroke engine should pass through four different strokes to complete one cycle so as to produce power. Here they are:

Intake stroke:

Starting from "Top Dead Center" (TDC), and zero degrees of rotation, the piston moves down the cylinder.

As the piston moves, it creates a vacuum and the intake valve opens, sucking air with fuel into the cylinder.

On carbureted engines, and on port and throttle body injected motors, the fuel comes in with the air, while on direct injected motors it is squirted directly into the cylinder.

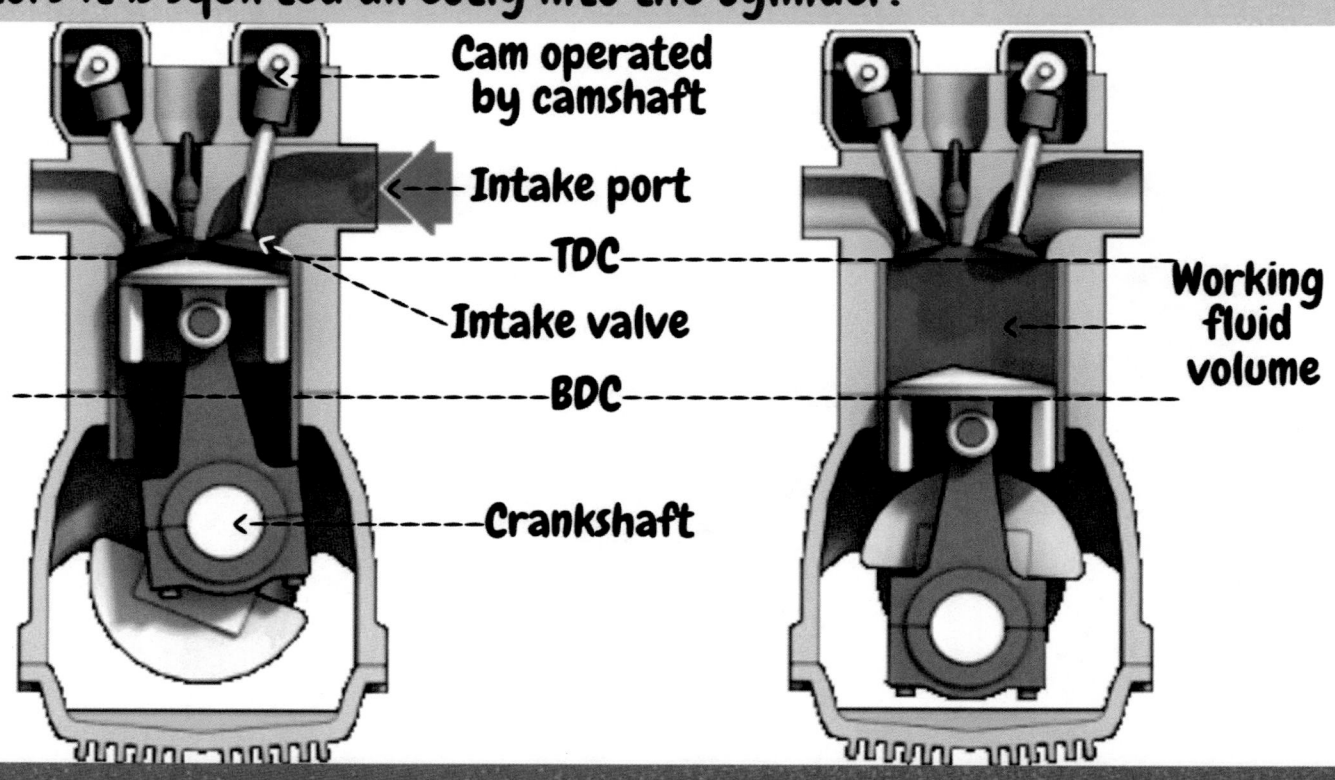

Compression Stroke:

At the end of the intake stroke, both inlet and exhaust valves are closed.

The inertial action of the crankshaft in turn lifts the piston which compresses the mixture.

The ratio of the combustion chamber volume, before and after compression, is called the compression ratio. Typically, the value is approximately 9:1 in spark ignition engines and 15:1 in diesel engines.

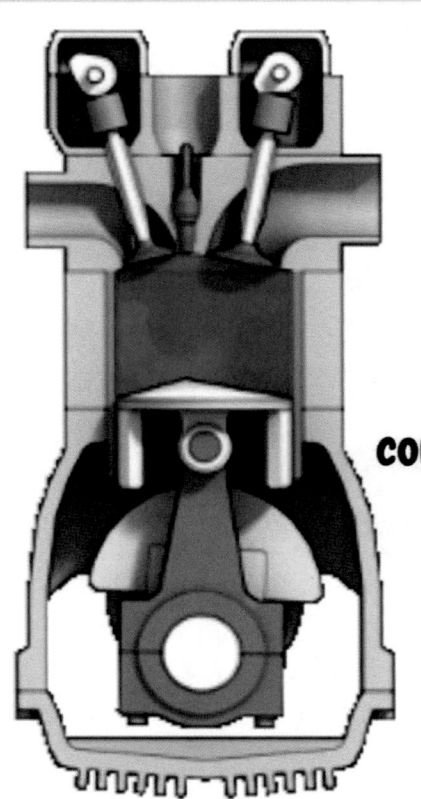
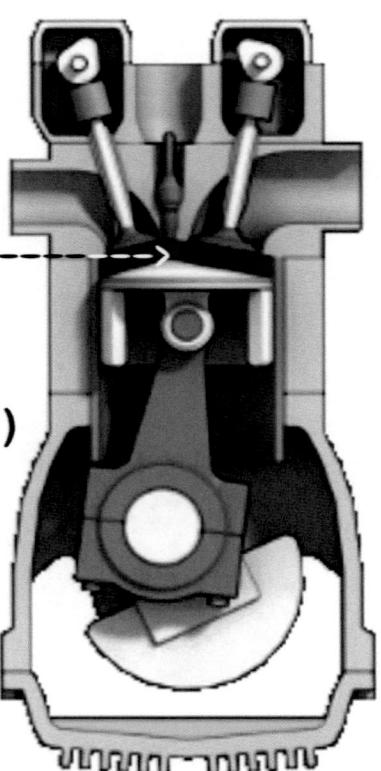

Combustion chamber

compression ratio = $(V + Vc / Vc)$

Vc = volume of combustion chamber

V = Working fluid volume.

Power Stroke:

This is where all the magic happens! The spark plug fires igniting the mixture, as the piston is at the top of the stroke.

The resultant explosion moves the piston rapidly back down the cylinder, turning the crankshaft, and making the car go.

In a diesel engine, there is no spark, the mixture just spontaneously ignites at the right moment due to the heat of compression.

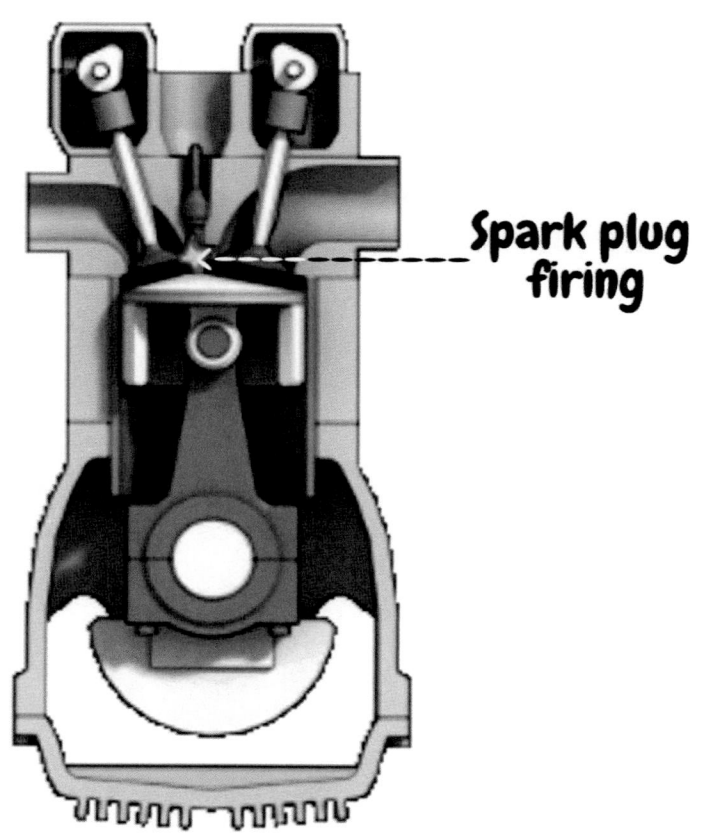

Spark plug firing

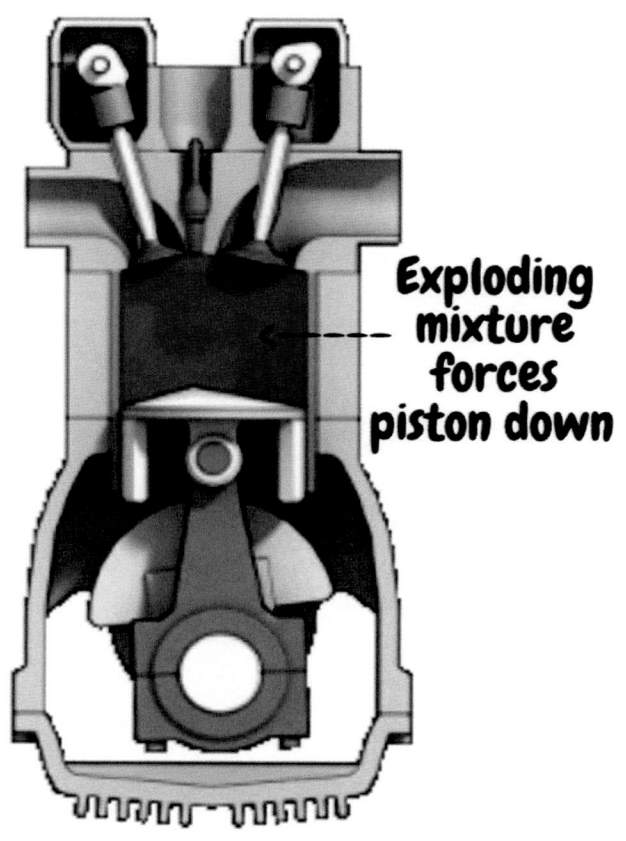

Exploding mixture forces piston down

Exhaust Stroke:

The piston moves back up the cylinder because of the momentum produced during the power stroke and the weight of the flywheel (in a single cylinder motor), or due to firing of the other cylinders.

The exhaust valve opens, and instead of compressing the burned gases, they are pushed out into the exhaust port.

As the piston gets close to TDC again, the exhaust valve starts to close, and the intake starts to open, for a small period called "overlap" where the escaping exhaust creates suction that helps pull air in via the intake valve opening.

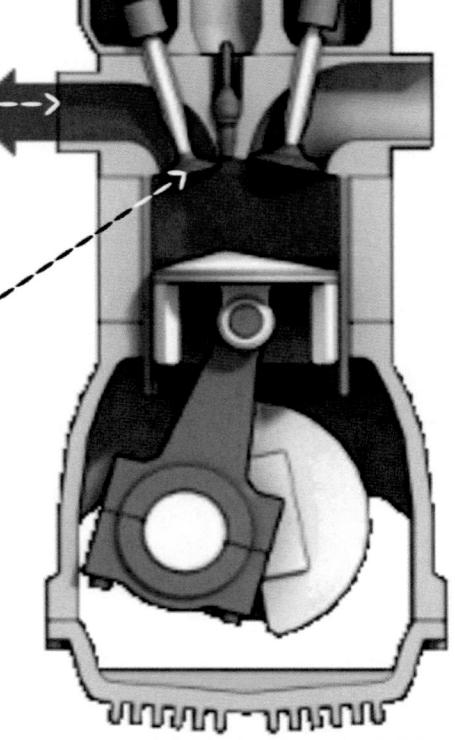

Exhaust port

Exhaust valve

The cycle then starts again, with the piston moving down on another intake stroke.

Camshafts and Crankshafts

Camshaft and crankshaft gears are connected by a timing chain (similar to a bicycle chain).

To control combustion, they must be indexed (aligned to manufacturer's specifications)in order to work in perfect harmony, called valve timing.

During, the four-stroke combustion cycle, (intake, compression, power and exhaust) the crankshaft turns twice – moving each piston up and down twice – while the camshaft turns once.

This makes each valve open one time for every two crankshaft revolutions in relation to the piston.

In this manner, only the intake valve(s) will open on the intake stroke, both valves remain closed during the compression and combustion strokes, and only the exhaust valve(s) opens during the exhaust stroke.

Firing order

The firing order of an internal combustion engine is the sequence of ignition for the cylinders (Power stroke).

In a spark ignition (e.g. gasoline/petrol) engine, the firing order corresponds to the order in which the spark plugs are operated.
In a Diesel engine, the firing order corresponds to the order in which fuel is injected into each cylinder.

Four-stroke engines must also time the valve openings relative to the firing order, as the valves do not open and close on every stroke.
Firing order affects the vibration, sound and evenness of power output from the engine.

The firing order heavily influences the crankshaft design.

For this inline-4 engine, 1-3-4-2 could be a valid firing order.

cylinder #1 will be the first to fire or generate power. Next up will be cylinder #3 followed by cylinder #4 and then finally cylinder #2.

Common firing orders

Straight-four Cylinder engines typically use a firing order of 1-3-4-2, however some British engines used a firing order of 1-2-4-3.

Straight-five Cylinder engines typically use a firing order of 1-2-4-5-3, in order to minimize the primary vibration.

Straight-six engines typically use a firing order of 1-5-3-6-2-4, which results in perfect primary and secondary balance.

V6 engines with an angle of 90 degrees between the cylinder banks have used a firing orders of R1-L2-R2-L3 L1-R3 or R1-L3-R3-L2-R2- L1,Several V6 engines with an angle of 60 degrees have used a firing order of R1-L1-R2-L2-R3-L3.

V8 engines use various firing orders, even using different firing orders between engines from the same manufacturer.

This V6 engine with an angle of 90 degrees between the cylinder banks,

use a firing order of R1-L2-R2-L3-L1-R3.

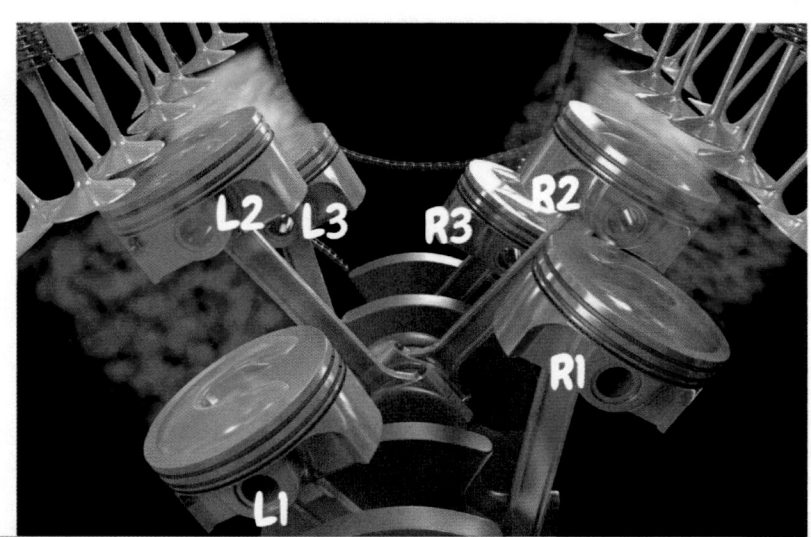

Example of 4 inline cylinder:

with firing order 1-3-4-2:

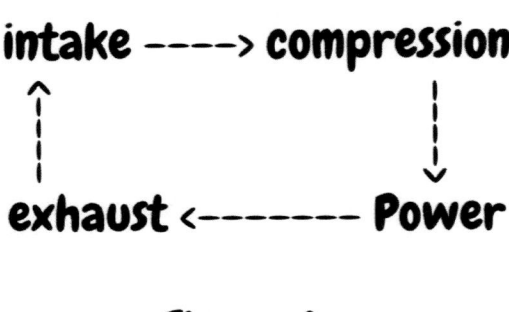

intake ----> compression

exhaust <------- Power

Figure 1

The 720 degrees of crankshaft rotation have been broken into 180-degree intervals to aid illustrating.

cylinder #1 starts off with the power stroke.

Since the firing order is 1-3-4-2, the next cylinder to fire will be cylinder #3.

#Cylinder	Crankshaft rotation in degrees
	180
1	Power
2	Exhaust
3	Compression
4	Intake

It follows from Figure 1, that if cylinder #1 is on the power stroke and cylinder #3 is the next to fire, it should be on the stroke before the power stroke because it is preparing to fire after cylinder #1.

This is the compression stroke – read figure 1 in a direction opposite to the arrows' direction, counterclockwise.

Cylinder #4 which fires after cylinder #3 should be two strokes behind the power stroke on cylinder #1. Examining Figure 1 again should help deduce that cylinder #4 is on the intake stroke.

Now, cylinder #2 should be 3 strokes behind the power stroke on cylinder #1. That would put cylinder #2 on the exhaust stroke, All of this happens in the first 180 degrees of crankshaft rotation.

In the next 180 degrees of crankshaft rotation (360 degrees),cylinder #3 enters the power stroke.

#Cylinder	Crankshaft rotation in degrees	
	180	360
1	Power	Exhaust
2	Exhaust	Intake
3	Compression	Power
4	Intake	Compression

Cylinder #4 is now on the compression stroke, cylinder #2 is on the intake stroke and cylinder #1 is, as expected, on the exhaust stroke to expel exhaust gases produced from the power stroke which is just completed.

In the next 180 degrees of crankshaft rotation (540 degrees), cylinder #4 enters the power stroke.

#Cylinder	Crankshaft rotation in degrees		
	180	360	540
1	Power	Exhaust	Intake
2	Exhaust	Intake	Compression
3	Compression	Power	Exhaust
4	Intake	Compression	Power

Cylinder #2 is now on the compression stroke, cylinder #1 is on the intake stroke and cylinder #3 is, as expected, on the exhaust stroke to expel exhaust gases produced from the power stroke which is just completed.

In the final 180 degrees of crankshaft rotation (720 degrees), cylinder #2 enters the power stroke.

#Cylinder	Crankshaft rotation in degrees			
	180	360	540	720
1	Power	Exhaust	Intake	Compression
2	Exhaust	Intake	Compression	Power
3	Compression	Power	Exhaust	Intake
4	Intake	Compression	Power	Exhaust

Cylinder #1 is now on the compression stroke, cylinder #3 is on the intake stroke, and cylinder #4 is, as expected, on the exhaust stroke to expel exhaust gases produced from the power stroke it just completed.

In the final 180 degrees (720 degrees), notice that cylinder 1 is back on the compression stroke, ready to start the entire process again as it moves from the compression stroke to the power stroke.

This figure illustrates a complete firing order with cylinders arranged in the proper firing order this time. This arrangement makes it easier to see how the cylinders fire every 180 degrees in accordance with the designated firing order.

#Cylinder	Crankshaft rotation in degrees			
	180	360	540	720
1	Power	Exhaust	Intake	Compression
3	Compression	Power	Exhaust	Intake
4	Intake	Compression	Power	Exhaust
2	Exhaust	Intake	Compression	Power

In a vehicle with a manual transmission, the flywheel is attached to the engine's crankshaft, therefore rotating according to the engine speed. A clutch sits between the flywheel and the transmission input shaft, controlling whether the transmission is connected to the engine.

When the engine is running and the clutch is engaged, the flywheel spins the clutch plate and hence the transmission.

Transmission

Internal-combustion engines run at high speeds, so a reduction in gearing is necessary to transmit power to the drive wheels, which turn much more slowly.

The gearbox provides a selection of gears for different driving conditions: standing start, climbing a hill, or cruising on level surfaces.

The lower the gear, the slower the road wheels turn in relation to the engine speed.

A transmission is another name for the car's gearbox, the component that turns the engine's power into something the car can use. Simply, without it, you'd sit in your car with the engine running but going nowhere.

The function of any transmission is transferring engine power to the driveshaft and rear wheels (or axle half shafts and front wheels in a front-wheel-drive vehicle).

Gears inside the transmission change the vehicle's drive-wheel speed and torque.

Modern cars with manual transmissions have five or six forward speeds and one reverse, as well as a neutral position.

The gear lever, operated by the driver, is connected to a series of selector rods on the top or the side of the gearbox.

The selector rods lie in parallel with shafts carrying the gears.

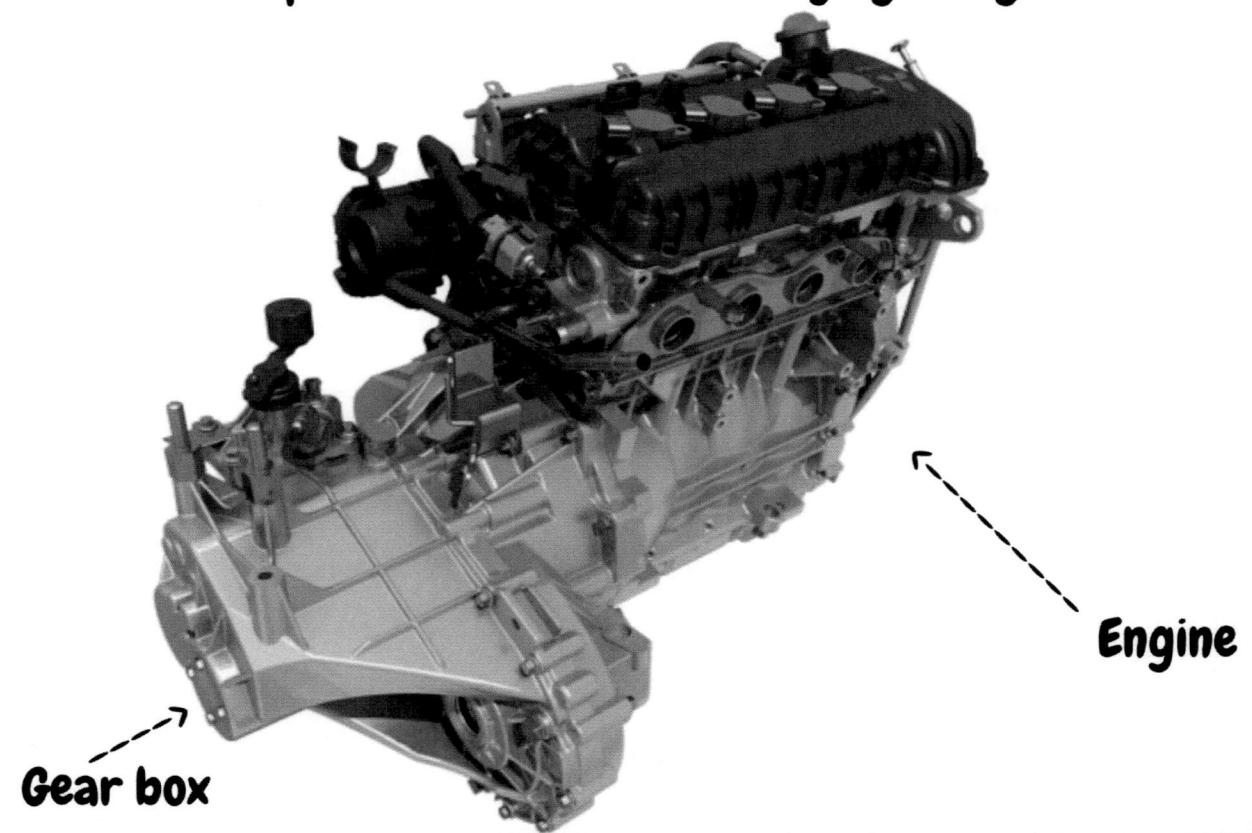

Engine

Gear box

Fuel

Fuel: A fuel is any material that can be made to react with other substances so that it releases energy as heat energy or to be used for work.

A vehicle's fuel system comprises components that deliver fuel from the tank to the engine, including a fuel pump, fuel lines, a fuel-pressure regulator, fuel filter and fuel injectors.

Fuel system components are built to last, so the fuel filter is the only part that's likely to require replacement on a schedule.

Fuel tank: The maximum distance a combustion-engine powered car with a full tank can cover is the product of the tank capacity and its fuel efficiency (as in miles per gallon), For most compact cars, the capacity is in the range 45-65 litres (12-17 US gal) SUVs and trucks tend to have considerably larger fuel tanks.

A fuel pump is a component that transfers liquid from the fuel tank to the carburetor of the internal combustion engine.

A pressure regulator is a valve that controls the pressure of a fluid or gas to a desired value.

A fuel filter is a filter in a fuel line that remove dirt and rust particles from the fuel, and is normally made into cartridges containing a filter paper.

They are found in most internal combustion engines.

A carburetor is a device that mixes air and fuel for internal combustion engines through valves, in the proper air-fuel ratio for combustion (mixing them together in different amounts for different driving condition).

Additional Information

The engine is the heart of your car, it is built to convert energy from the heat of burning gasoline into mechanical work, or torque (force). That torque is applied to turn the road wheels.

What powers those pistons up and down are thousands of controlled explosions (chain of reactions) each minute, which achieve that objective of setting in motion by a spark, which ignites a mixture of petrol vapor and compressed air inside a momentarily sealed cylinder and causes it to burn rapidly.

That is why the machine is called an internal combustion engine, As the mixture burns, it expands, providing power to drive the car. Engines need air (namely oxygen) to burn fuel.

During the intake stroke, the valves open to allow the piston to act like a syringe, as it moves downward, drawing in ambient air through the engine's intake system. When the piston reaches the bottom of its stroke, the intake valves close, effectively sealing the cylinder for the compression stroke, which is in the opposite direction as the intake stroke. The upward movement of the piston compresses the intake charge.

Made in the USA
Las Vegas, NV
31 October 2023

79925340R00026